Lessons from Audre Lorde's *The Uses of Anger*

UCONN Women's, Gender, and Sexuality Studies at 50

Featuring
Audre Lorde,
M. Jacqui Alexander, and
Beverly Guy-Sheftall

Introduced and organized by
Jane Anna Gordon, Briona Simone Jones,
Elva Orozco Mendoza, and **Sherry Zane**

Cover art by **Sula Gordon**

Daraja Press

UCONN
Women's Gender & Sexualities Studies

Published by Daraja Press
https://darajapress.com
Wakefield, Quebec, Canada

© Daraja Press 2024
All rights reserved

ISBN 9781998309023

Library and Archives Canada Cataloguing in Publication

Title: Lessons from Audre Lorde's The uses of anger : UCONN Women's, Gender and Sexuality Studies at 50 / Audre Lorde, Jane Anna Gordon, Briona Simone Jones, Elva Orozco Mendoza, Sherry Zane.
Other titles: Audre Lorde's The uses of anger
Names: Container of (work): Lorde, Audre. Uses of anger.
Description: Includes bibliographical references.
Identifiers: Canadiana 20240318668 | ISBN 9781998309023 (softcover)
Subjects: LCSH: Feminism and racism. | LCSH: National Women's Studies Association. | LCSH: University of Connecticut. Women's, Gender, and Sexuality Studies Program.
Classification: LCC HQ1150 .L47 2024 | DDC 305.42—dc23

CONTENTS

Lessons from *The Uses of Anger*: UCONN WGSS at 50   1
Jane Anna Gordon, Elva Orozco Mendoza, and Sherry Zane

The Uses of Anger: Women Responding to Racism   24
Audre Lorde

To Grow through Genealogy: An Interview with   34
M. Jacqui Alexander and Beverly Guy-Sheftall
Briona Simone Jones

Contributor Biographies   45

Lessons from The Uses of Anger: UCONN WGSS at 50

Jane Anna Gordon, Elva Orozco Mendoza, Sherry Zane

Our Inheritance, Our Responsibility

Like many Women's Studies units across the United States, ours was born of struggles for social transformation and liberation in the 1960s and 1970s. Proudly marked by these origins, the Women's, Gender, and Sexuality Studies (WGSS) program at the University of Connecticut (UCONN) is a dynamic intellectual unit with a long-shared tradition of social justice initiatives and committed mentorship in and beyond the classroom. Defined by critical methods of inquiry, our research and curriculum are socially engaged and focused on developing compelling analyses of and responses to global problems, including ableism, antiblackness, antisemitism, coloniality, homophobia, Islamophobia, sexism, transphobia, and xenophobia, that foster and sustain systems of domination and exclusion. To be based at UCONN is to be based at a predominantly white, public land-grant institution of higher education.[1] This space, which includes our WGSS program, is crucial to the context in which Caribbean-American poet and social theorist Audre Lorde first delivered her famous speech, "The Uses of Anger: Women Responding to Racism," which we are reprinting here in celebration of WGSS's 50th anniversary.

In the WGSS tradition of reckoning with difficult truths, we would be remiss not to acknowledge that, even as we join together to celebrate fifty

---

1 "Land-grant" means that the federal government allowed so-called "unclaimed" public land to be sold for profit that would be given to existing colleges within each state. Universities benefitted from this scheme because the government dispossessed, murdered, and forcibly removed Native Americans from their land to live on reservations. Many indigenous people refer to land-grant institutions as "land-grab" universities, through which nearly eleven million acres of Indigenous land were stolen by over 160 violence-backed treaties and land seizures, that decimated approximately 250 tribes, bands, and communities. For more, see Lee, Ahtone, Pearce, Goodluck, McGhee, Leff, Lanpher, and Salinas, 2021.

years, we do so on the original homelands of Indigenous peoples, most of whom were forcibly removed through acts of genocide and dispossession. We recognize that people's lives in these spaces still often rely on continued resource extraction and many are subject to persistent racial segregation, surveillance, and policing as part of an ongoing settler-colonial project. In the recent past, our communities have been marked by many, profound losses and, as we write, we face major fiscal disinvestment in our institution's future.

The current institutional arrangements and status of WGSS within the university are the result of prior historical conditions, many of which arose out of crisis, protest, and public concern. Three women professors designed and taught the first Women's Studies courses at UCONN during the 1971-1972 academic year. As Aimee Loiselle recounts:

> The official formation and funding of the Women's Studies Program occurred after two years of persistent organizing, activism, and lobbying that utilized several overlapping tactics. These included formal institutional proposals, calls for enforcement of Title VII of the Civil Rights Act, negotiations with the administration, the federal affirmative action criteria, student demonstrations, community outreach, and a class action lawsuit. (2017-2018, 1)[2]

Those who organized and lobbied promised that Women's Studies would create more inclusive course offerings and exciting new interdisciplinary scholarship that prioritized illuminating historical and ongoing struggles against systemic violence.

Yet, while WGSS has fulfilled such promises, consistently producing exemplary results, until now, we have remained bound by the constraints of our inception. Despite the initial small number of faculty – one Board of Trustees Distinguished jointly-appointed professor, one jointly-appointed tenured professor, and four contingent, in-residence faculty – WGSS continued to provide far more general education seats per semester than do significantly larger units and has many more majors and minors. In 2023, the WGSS minor ranked #10 out of 105 minors across the entire University. WGSS recently won an Andrew W. Mellon Foundation Grant, in part

---

[2] Loiselle conducted this research while a PhD student as part of a proposal to UCONN's Special Collections to reorganize their papers to foreground the details of the WGSS program's development.

because we met the criteria of being a small program with a substantial number of graduated majors in the Humanities. Even former UCONN President, Tom Katsouleas recognized WGSS in his inaugural speech as providing students with life-transformative experiences. Yet, without the ability to tenure, WGSS has relied on joint appointments, contingent faculty, and an administration's willingness to invest.

A recent moment of substantial investment occurred in response to tragic circumstances. The murders of Black-Americans Breonna Taylor on March 13, 2020 and George Floyd on May 25, 2020 triggered a surge of promises of support for greater diversity, equity, and inclusion across colleges and universities in the United States.[3] As more Americans became aware of the long violent history of racism in policing through social media outlets, University administrators scrambled to show support for the principles and demands of Black Lives Matter,[4] creating and filling new positions for chief diversity officers, and announcing their commitment to increasing their efforts to hire and retain more faculty, staff, and students who identified as Black, Indigenous, or People of Color. Former UCONN President Tom Katsouleas (2019–2021), former UCONN Provost Carl Lejuez (2020–2022), and former UCONN College of

---

[3] The events of 2020 had clear precursors – and any attempt to understand the current crisis still requires a reckoning with the recent past. In fact, Lorde's poem titled, "Power" published in 1978, describes how a 37-year-old white policeman was set free after murdering a Black ten-year-old child by a jury comprised of his peers and one Black Woman. Lorde writes,

> Today that 37 year old white man
> with 13 years of police forcing
> was set free
> by eleven white men who said they were satisfied
> justice had been done
> and one Black Woman who said
> "They convinced me" meaning
> they had dragged her 4'10" black Woman's frame
> over the hot coals
> of four centuries of white male approval
> until she let go
> the first real power she ever had
> and lined her own womb with cement
> to make a graveyard for our children.

[4] In 2013, in response to the acquittal of Trayvon Martin's murderer, George Zimmerman, three radical Black organizers – Alicia Garza, Patrisse (Khan) Cullors, and Opal (Ayo) Tometi – created a Black-centered political will and movement-building project called #BlackLivesMatter. "The Black Lives Matter Foundation, Inc is a global organization in the US, UK, and Canada, whose mission is to eradicate white supremacy and build local power to intervene in violence inflicted on Black communities by the state and vigilantes. By combating and countering acts of violence, creating space for Black imagination and innovation, and centering Black joy, we are winning immediate improvements in our lives." https://blacklivesmatter.com

Liberal Arts and Sciences Dean Juli Wade (2019–2023) all voiced desires to produce systemic change at the University.[5]

As part of this effort, in the Fall of 2020, Dean Wade announced a competition, inviting proposals for cluster hires of jointly appointed faculty whose work would contribute to addressing bias and racism. These clusters were expected to augment hires from the previous year that had focused on Native American and Indigenous Studies and on racialized health disparities. Several faculty from across departments, many of whom were or are affiliated with WGSS, authored a proposal titled "Catalyzing Antiracist and Decolonial Futures" (CARDF). Although the authors requested six lines, with at least two hires who would enter with tenure and seniority, they were awarded four tenure-track hiring lines. Several other hiring projects were also chosen, including one focused on "big data" and the environment, and single-line hires in Communication, Journalism, and History.

In a job ad that elicited approximately 500 applicants, the committee identified CARDF scholarship as

> Rooted in intersectional struggles against dehumanization, denigration, and dispossession and for decolonization and liberation. Anti-racist and anti-bias scholarship thus involves the active work of dismantling systems of oppression, including larger systems of thought, through generating reparative alternatives, modes of justice and healing, and visions of transformative futures.

The CARDF hiring committee, in ongoing conversation with each of the partnering departments and units, were especially excited about candidates whose research was indisputably exemplary but did not fit neatly in existing institutional configurations. They hoped that, as a critical mass, such new scholars would help existing faculty to build a new transdisciplinary entity on campus, one that better reflected emergent directions of scholarly endeavor.

Three of the four CARDF hires and the candidate in Communication chose WGSS as their joint appointment.. This transformed the program overnight. In addition to the immediate, significant increase in faculty teaching in WGSS, the research they had produced included

---

5 It is worth mentioning that none of these administrators remain in these positions today.

an award-winning anthology of Black lesbian thought and scholarly articles on maternal activism in Latin America as a response to feminicide, Black feminist epistemology and #MeToo, and transnational social media activism. This combined with the output of existing faculty, which recently included a monograph on care work and disability and an omnibus companion to Women's, Gender, and Sexuality Studies.

This spring 2024, WGSS is actively working toward becoming a new department, together with American Studies, Asian and Asian American Studies, and Native American and Indigenous Studies. For the first time in the history of all four programs, members of the new entity will be able to hire, tenure, promote, and award merit to faculty independently. Many of our faculty and staff face a hostile racial climate and social isolation to which UConn administrators have yet to offer structural solutions.. Departmental status is one way to offer more institutional support so our faculty can do the coalition-building Lorde demanded of us.

With gratitude to all the students, faculty, staff, community members, and administrators who fought for WGSS over the years, we invite you to celebrate and reflect on these developments as ways that WGSS at UCONN, like the National Women's Studies Association (NWSA), worked to heed the necessary challenges that Lorde outlined in 1981 at Storrs.

As Lorde did then, we find ourselves facing multiple manifestations of an ascendant domestic and transnational right-wing unapologetic of its calls for violence. Whether renewed attacks on abortion access, attempts to ban the teaching of critical race feminism, continued assaults on transgender people and LGBTQIA+ movements in conjunction with anti-migrant and racist perspectives across the U.S., or seemingly contagious militarization, war, and policies of genocide globally, Lorde's challenge for how to nurture, build, and sustain tenacious progressive solidarities continues. *What can we learn, re-learn, or re-VISION about our responsibility for this inherited history, its legacy, and our future from Lorde's transformative praxis?*

The Response to Racism is Anger

> *My response to racism is anger. I have lived with that anger, ignoring it, feeding upon it, learning to use it before it laid my visions to waste, for most of my life. Once I did it in silence, afraid of the weight. My fear of anger taught me nothing. Your fear of that anger will teach you nothing, also.* (2007, 124)

In recent years, we have witnessed renewed calls for women to embrace anger as a source of power (Cep 2018). These voices have Lorde's "The Uses of Anger" to thank for charting an innovative scholarly and poetic terrain that theorizes anger as much more empowering and liberating than conventional discussions of the term typically allow.

Lorde's essay redefined anger productively, approaching it as an epistemological tool igniting a desire for self and collective liberation. The result was a remarkable critical reflection that laid the groundwork for deconstructing broader systems of oppression, particularly, heteronormativity, heteropatriarchy, institutionalized racial poverty, racial capitalism, and white privilege. Lorde's essay moved with precision, centering Black women's struggles in a world built around the use – and abuse – of racialized people subjected to systematic dehumanization.

Lorde's prose delivered a bold message: anger is not a sign of (Black women's) weakness of character nor is it an individual or psychological defect. Instead, it is a response to entrenched racism, antiblack violence, unjust institutions, and the refusal of white (liberal) feminists to engage in an honest conversation about these problems, accepting instead historical distortions about Women of Color's alleged differences.[6] By defining anger in this way, Lorde not only showed that "rage is a legitimate political emotion" (Cooper 2018, 5), she also established herself as a formidable contributor to Black feminist thought and one of its most assiduous supporters.

---

6 The term "Women of Color" emerged in the U.S. in 1977 at the National Women's Conference sponsored by then President Jimmy Carter. To address the inadequacies of the organizers' three-page minority women's plank, Black women brought a "Black women's agenda" to the meeting. After hearing its content, the rest of the minoritized women wanted to be included. Unable then to call it the "Black" women's platform, they agreed to refer to it as that of the "Women of Color." Loretta J. Ross (2011) explained that the aim had not been to emphasize biological differences, but to make a statement of solidarity or a public commitment to work collaboratively among women who had been minoritized.

"The Uses of Anger" vindicated the knowledge Black women produced based on their lived experiences, imbuing it with scholarly and practical authority. The problem with anger, Lorde reminded us, is neither that (Black) women cannot control it nor that it is useless and disruptive (Lorde 2007). The problem is, rather, that white supremacist ideologies, including those that wave a feminist flag, demonize and delegitimize anger to avoid responding to state violence deployed against Black people and other racialized groups. This brute inhumanity not only denies their rights to exist, but also to flourish and care for one another.

As a Black woman, poet, lesbian, feminist, warrior, and mother – identities that she lived into and deeply cherished – Lorde regularly experienced racism firsthand. Survival for her, then, depended on deciphering racism's inner logic as constitutive of broader violent structures. Decoding the roots and effects of racism was also crucial to understanding how Black women's survival strategies, whether individual or collective, could inform the creation of anti-racist coalitions. In short, anger could, for Lorde, be a transformative catalyst for change. But exactly what kind of change can anger generate? Who are the 'agents' and 'subjects' of change? More crucially, how is racial anger mobilized for transformation?

Racism, as Lorde defined it, is "[t]he belief in the inherent superiority of one race over all others and thereby the right to dominance, manifest and implied" (2007, 124). This seemingly simple definition calls our attention to 'belief systems' that distort reality to depict some groups as inherently better than others and base their practices of domination on those distortions. Lorde's definition does not link racism to colonial domination explicitly. Nevertheless, her critique applies to colonialism as much as it does to racial capitalism to the extent that these interconnected structures mobilize homophobic, racist, sexist, and xenophobic justifications to reinforce systems of privilege and inequity that prevent transformative alternatives to current structures. As Lorde warns in "The Master's Tools Will Never Dismantle the Master's House," "What does it mean when the tools of a racist patriarchy are used to examine the fruits of that same patriarchy? It means that only the narrowest parameters of change are possible and allowable" (2007, 110-11).

Lorde further remarks, "We are not here as women examining racism in a political and social vacuum. We operate in the teeth of a system for which racism and sexism are primary, established, and necessary props of profit" (2007, 128). Racism and sexism, in other words, are instruments of capitalist dispossession. As such, these instruments perpetuate, rather than remedying, the suffering of Black and People of Color. But, as the previous quote rightly suggests, racism does not stand-alone; it belongs to a larger web of affective, political, and socioeconomic structures that mask historically constructed inequalities to naturalize and make them appear inevitable.

Thus, when expressed as an indictment of personal and institutional oppressions, anger becomes, according to Lorde, "a powerful source of energy serving progress and change" (2007, 127). Crucially, for her, change requires anti-heteronormativity, anti-patriarchy, and anti-racist action beyond mere "academic rhetoric" (2007, 129). Change, in Lorde's own words, "[does not] mean a simple switch of positions or a temporary lessening of tensions, nor the ability to smile or feel good. I am speaking of a basic and radical alteration in those assumptions underlining our lives" (2007, 127). As this passage suggests, Lordean change is structural. It aims to permanently and substantially transform dominant epistemic frameworks that define certain groups as inferior to keep them oppressed. Understood in this way, change must alter the affective dispositions, material conditions, oppression, poverty, and violence facing Black, lesbian, gay men, and impoverished women.

Confined to academic spaces and discussions, change, in Lorde's view, remains inconsequential; it supports the status quo as it naturalizes racial inequality. By contrast, radical change works to dismantle capitalist, class, gender, racial, and sexual oppression in all their forms, for, as Lorde notes, "I am not free while any woman is unfree, even when her shackles are very different from my own. And I am not free as long as one person of color remains chained. Nor is any one of you" (2007, 132-3).

As such, change is everybody's responsibility. Lorde urged others to recognize interlocking systems of oppression and the need to organize collectively. During Black History Month in 1982, Lorde delivered a speech at Harvard University titled "Learning from the 60s." In it she urged students to engage in effective coalition-building, noting "There is no such thing as a single-issue struggle because we do not live single-issue lives" (2007, 138). Systemic change can only happen if we "commit ourselves to some future that can include each other and to work towards that future with the particular strengths of our individual identities" (Ibid.). Lorde's "The Uses of Anger", in conjunction with many of her other speeches and writings, can be understood as a call to practice allyship. However, she makes clear that such coalition politics is not easy. At the very least, it requires sustained critical self-reflection and willingness to consider (and reconsider) how one's own position can, even unintentionally, harm others.

Repertoires of Evasion: Racialized Gendered Socializations

If anger is so vital a resource, why does it remain so demeaned and devalued – an emotion so many women feel compelled to diligently suppress and disavow? If NWSA sought to address racism, beginning within its ranks, and the most legitimate response to racism was anger, what was the internal response to this anger?

White Women's Modes of Evasion

Lorde's particular focus here, given her audience, was white women – and all the distinct and overlapping ways they, in the main, evaded rather than faced expressions of anger. After all, as Lorde wrote, anger is, in a sense, a gift. "If I speak to you in anger, at least I have spoken to you: I have not put a gun to your head and shot you down in the street" (2007, 130). Those at whom anger was channeled were addressed, not physically attacked. Lorde added, with historical reference, "I have not looked at your bleeding sister's body and asked, 'What did she do to deserve it?'" as two white women responded to Mary Church Terrell's recounting in 1921 of the lynching of a pregnant Black woman whose baby was torn from her body (Ibid.). Still, few, if any girls or women, had been guided in engaging, let alone engaging constructively, with anger. Consistently, white women's socialization was *especially lacking*.

If both anger and "attendant fears" could facilitate personal and political growth, guilt and defensiveness were "bricks in a wall against which we all flounder," serving "none of our futures" (2007, 124). Such defensiveness took – and takes – many forms, examples of which Lorde shared generously. The catalog of all-too-familiar tactics of evasion, which Lorde noted was far shorter than it might have been, was still seemingly interminable.

Drawn directly from white feminist university settings, these avoidant strategies included, in a way that echoed the insights of Anna Julia Cooper's *A Voice from the South*, a fear of the histories that Black people – especially Black women – brought with them, wherever and whenever they entered. In a narcissism that simply recentered them, one white woman pleaded with a Black woman speaker not to be *too harsh*, as if what was at stake was not the message but its delivery. Patronizingly, several white women admitted to preferring to talk of racism with non-Black Women of Color who were framed as less potentially harsh than their Black women counterparts. In a gathering aimed at interracial understanding, one woman measured success by Women of Color taking pains to understand *her*. The failures only continued in consistently expecting Women of Color to initiate and sustain anti-racist praxis – they claimed not to be able to address racism if no Women of Color were present – and framed themselves as permanently ill-equipped to teach Black or Women of Color's writing, rather than as responsible for learning to do so.

When the same white feminist women turned inward, to examine their own relationship to racism, they wanted to deal tenderly with "little colored children," "the beloved nursemaid," and the "occasional second-grade classmate [of color]" (2007, 125). Not with fellow women of equal standing in the now or with the thick antiblackness, imbibed with laughter, in "children's stories" or gestures like a white mother who placed a handkerchief below where her daughter would sit because Lorde had recently been there. And when contemporary manifestations of antiblack socialization appeared irrefutably, with, for instance, a small white girl calling Lorde's little daughter a "baby maid," the white mother shushed but did not correct the child – suggesting she was more embarrassed than concerned about the differential life expectations her daughter had already internalized. What is more, shushing attached "terror and dis-ease" to the now-grown white daughter's memory of what transpired and its subsequent invocation in ways that only contributed to the challenge of having the very kinds of conversation NWSA sought to foster but did not fully prepare for (2007, 126).

Lorde asks if such women really seek a dialogue about racism. She is skeptical given the repeated failures to pay attention to the actual lives of the women who were supposed to meaningfully converge in a meeting like the NWSA conference. If the organizers truly aimed to stage conversations that considered the full range of challenges posed to all women, it could have waived registration fees for those who wished to participate but lacked funds. Failure to treat such concerns as priorities was an example of settling for "discussing life within the closed circuits of the academy" (2007, 127) while claiming to consider all women's lives in their full complexity.

Undergirding these modes of evasion, which, in Lorde's account, "creat[e] a mood of hopelessness" and "[stand] in the way of trusting communication and action" (2007, 131), was guilt. While guilt can occasionally, through self-analysis, lead to growth, it more typically "[buys] time" when urgent "clear choices" (2007, 130) are what is needed. Lorde describes guilt as a preoccupation with one's past inaction instead of dealing with Black and Women of Color's present expressions of anger. This allows white women to be complicit by ignoring and dismissing any effort to address systemic racism.

Lorde acknowledges that most women have not learned to face anger directly in the eyes. She describes white women who "become filled with fury" when hearing a racist comment but who "remain silent because they are afraid" (2007, 127). The anger seething within them is potentially explosive – "like an undetonated device" – but it is often fundamentally misdirected. Indeed, Lorde writes, with a sense of familiarity, that it is usually "hurled at the first woman of Color who talks about racism" (Ibid.).[7]

When largely white women's consciousness-raising groups made the expression of anger a priority of discussion, their focus was on "the world of men" (2007, 130). They rarely considered that, as white women, they

---

7 Lorde describes how a white woman moved by rage turned to her with a "blank look in her eyes" when Lorde asked what *she* would do with her anger (2007, 125). Lorde states plainly and pedagogically, "I do not exist to feel her anger for her" (Ibid.). For Lorde, feeling one's own anger is necessary to avoiding self-annihilation.

also partake in the system of oppression, even if unwittingly. As Lorde put it, "What woman here is so enamored of her own oppression that she cannot see her heelprint upon another woman's face?" (2007, 132). So enamored, they rarely focused on anger directed at each other or at them by Women of Color. Hence no "tools were developed to deal with other women's anger except to avoid it, deflect it, or flee from it under a blanket of guilt" (2007, 130).

Such deflection has deep roots as most women were raised to fear widely, broadly, and deeply. For starters, they were told to fear the many who might hurt or take advantage of them. And for women raised fearfully, wrote Lorde, "too often anger threatens annihilation" (2007, 131). If power is framed only as domination, wielded in varieties of "brute force" that women cannot withstand on their own, the lesson is clear: "our lives depended upon the good will of patriarchal power" (Ibid.). Anger from others "was to be avoided at all costs" (Ibid.). All that could follow from it was pain and judgment. After all, if one had elicited *their* anger, "we had been bad girls, come up lacking, not done what we were supposed to do" (Ibid.). The fault, of course, was *ours:* all women.

Lorde warns that "if we accept our powerlessness," first by conceding that power can only be exercised as brutality and second by believing that all we can do in the face of it is comply or surrender, "then, of course, any anger can destroy us" (Ibid.). But must or should we accept either of these terms? For those white women "who fear the anger of women of Color more than their own unscrutinized racist attitudes" (2007, 129), Lorde asks, is the fear that Women of Color catalyze in white women actually more threatening than *the ascendant woman-hatred* saturating everyone's lives? She does not explicitly mention the widely shared anger and fear on the part of conference attendees in response to the political rise, with then U.S. President Ronald Reagan, of a then-new Far Right and "Moral Majority," both of which sought to turn back all the strides that 1970s radical activism had made.[8] They envisioned doing so as an act of healthy and necessary restoration in ways now echoed in former

---

8 The Moral Majority was a U.S. political organization founded by Baptist minister Jerry Falwell Sr. and Paul Weyrich in 1979. A predominantly Southern organization of the Christian Right, it played a central role in mobilizing conservative Christians to secure U.S. Republican presidential victories during the 1980s. It officially disbanded in 1989 when Falwell saw its work, of assuring a solid place for the religious right in U.S. politics and the country, as having been achieved.

U.S. President Donald J. Trump's messaging about "making America great again."

If we can avoid deflection by demanding more of ourselves, facing anger can involve "the hard work of excavating honesty" (2007, 128). In a word, Lorde is asking that white women grow up and seize their potential power by reconceptualizing its meaning. After all, in a system in which racism and sexism are interwoven modes of profiteering, women, especially white women's responses, to racism can be dangerous (Ibid.). Lorde suggested that when white U.S. women framed racism as *their* society's problem, they denaturalized it, reframing it as a historical and human creation that can be eradicated. Turning "aside from the anger of Black women" because one is intimidated "is to award no one [new] power" (2007, 132). It preserves "racial blindness, the power of unaddressed privilege, unbreached, intact" (Ibid.). Such a turn led to Lorde's central diagnosis, that as oppressions are linked, they must be faced together in the pursuit of freedom.

Forms of Evasion among Women of Color, Specifically Black Women

It was two years later, in "Eye to Eye: Black Women, Hatred, and Anger," that Lorde wrote more extensively and explicitly about anger among Black women. In "The Uses of Anger," she turns briefly to "all her sisters of Color" who keep their "rage under harness," questioning whether the accusations are true that its expression would be "useless and disruptive" (2007, 127). She is clearly doubtful.

She explains how, as girls of color become women, they face repeated messages that they are of value only in service to a world in which they are repeatedly *unchosen*. She names the resulting "symphony of anger," or efforts to coordinate and orchestrate the constant legitimate feelings of fury required simply to live an ordinary life. Those who do not learn these difficult lessons *do not make it*. Indeed, Lorde writes, "part of [her] anger is always libation for [her] fallen sisters" (Ibid.). As such, it is a constant companion.

When Lorde reiterates, as do we, that anger is "loaded with information and energy" (2007, 127), she acknowledges that when she refers to Women of Color, she is not only speaking of Black women. Exemplifying the lesson she is trying to convey, Lorde writes that if a non-Black Woman of Color were angrily to call her out for subsuming her experience in a blackness with which she did not identify, it would be a waste not to learn from the correction, even if it is profoundly difficult to listen to a woman describe "an agony I do not share, or one to which I myself have contributed" (2007, 128).

Similarly, Lorde differentiates herself – as a Black lesbian whose children eat regularly because she works for and is paid by a university – while insisting that it would be her failure not to see her commonality with a lesbian mother of color who cannot find regular work or who does not have children "because her insides are rotted from home abortions and sterilization" (2007, 132), or who remains closeted out of need of a homophonic community's support. Such a woman may be terrified that Lorde's anger might make her own explode. To respond with evasive guilt, however, would be to buttress separation rather than clarifying that she – and therefore we – are not free, however distinct the shackles.

In "Eye to Eye," Lorde distinguishes the "middle-depth" relations between Black and white women, presumably those at work in a setting like the NWSA conference, from deeper ones between and among Black women. It was in the former, which held "true for office workers and political activists as well as lovers" (2007, 163), where she suggested anger could, in principle, pry open communication and real meeting. "[L]ess threatening than the tangle of unexplored needs and furies that face any two Black women who seek to engage each other directly," (2007, 163) if the former focused on racism in white people, the latter was a different battle, of "confront[ing] and wad[ing] through the racist constructs underlying our deprivation of each other" (2007, 164). Lorde concedes, "It is so much easier to express our anger in those middle depth relationships that do not threaten genuine self-exposure" (2007, 167).

Lorde prefaces these reflections with a different kind of assessment: "Before I can write about Black women's anger, I must write about the poisonous seepage of hatred that fuels that anger, and of the cruelty that is spawned when [Black women] meet" (2007, 146). She emphasizes that *she knows* other Black women are not the cause of the anger that "unleash[es] itself most tellingly against another Black woman at the least excuse"

(2007, 145) and that "the road to anger is paved with our unexpressed fear of each other's judgment" (2007, 169).

Sharing formative experiences of "that societal deathwish directed against us from the moment we were born Black and female in America," there was a toll of being "steeped in hatred – for our color, for our sex, for our effrontery in daring to presume we had any right to live" (Ibid.). Whether Lorde being assumed and patronized as "simple" by optometrists examining her very limited eyes or hurting as she looked at the grotesque pictures in *Little Black Sambo*, a book that made all her school peers laugh. Or the historical experimentation on Black women "out of a curiosity masquerading as science" (2007, 150) . . . Lorde asks, *"What other human being absorbs so much virulent hostility [several lifetimes of hatred] and still functions?"* (2007, 151, italics added)

At home, her light-skinned Grenadian mother never "talked about color," but her lighter sisters were always "well-behaved," "neat," and "quiet" while she was "rowdy," "sloppy," and "noisy." They were "good looking," while she was "dark" and "bad" and "mischievous" (2007, 149). Lorde asks pointedly, "Did *bad* mean *Black?* . . . . The endless scrubbing with lemon juice in the cracks and crevices of [her] ripening, darkening, body" suggested the answer was "yes" (Ibid.). If Lorde's mother taught her to survive, she also taught "isolation, fury, mistrust, self-rejection, and sadness" (2007, 149); to "fear [her] own Blackness" (2007, 165).[9] Before understanding "the hatred and despisal that embroidered [her] life . . . where that hatred came from, or why it was being heaped upon [her]" (2007, 146), Lorde assumed she was to blame. She "decided there must be something terribly wrong with [her] that inspired such contempt" (Ibid.).

Even if her mother made it clear that "outside shouldn't oughta be the way it was" (2007, 150), *it was.* Lorde describes being encircled by unexplained anger that "spilled out against whomever was closest that shared those hated selves" (2007, 150). Asking why she judged fellow Black women more critically than anyone else (2007, 145), she answers

---

9 Lorde's mother would say, "Don't trust white people because they mean us no good and don't trust anyone darker than you because their hearts are as Black as their faces" (2007, 165). Acknowledging that it was still painful to write all those years later, Lorde asked where that counsel left her, the darkest daughter?

that fueling the attack was "the face of [her] own self, unaccepted" (2007, 146).

Lorde suggests that for all their enveloping weight, it was easier to deal with external "racism and sexism than it [was] to deal with the results of those distortions internalized within our consciousness of ourselves and one another" (2007, 147). She describes how her anger would attach "itself in the strangest places. Upon those as powerless as [she]" (2007, 150). She knew her own anger intimately, like "the beat of [her] heart and taste of [her] spit" (2007, 153). *And it was far easier to be angry – or even furious – than to hurt or to yearn.* Lorde concedes, "Easier to crucify myself in you than to take on the threatening universe of whiteness by admitting that we are worth wanting each other" (Ibid.).

If Black women's literature was rich with dreams of deep connection and genuine communication (2007, 153), their realization required surmounting tremendous barriers. Doing so entailed candid and difficult self-analysis, exploring distancing anger and separating fear, rather than settling for "pretenses of connection, or for parodies of self-love" (Ibid.). [10] Absent such working through:

> We maintain a discreet distance between each other because that distance between us makes me less you, makes you less me. When there is no connection at all between people, then anger is a way of bringing them closer together.... But when there is a great deal of connectedness that is problematic or threatening or unacknowledged, then anger is a way of keeping people separate, of putting distance between us. (2007, 168)

Without loving oneself as a Black woman, one cannot love other Black women. To see one's own face in another is to encounter a "face we never stopped wanting at the same time as we try to obliterate it" (2007, 155). But the anger is "so huge and implacable, so corrosive, it must destroy what it most needs for its own solution, dissolution, resolution" (2007, 157). Lorde asks, "How often have I demanded from another Black woman what I had not dared to give myself – acceptance, faith, enough space to consider change?" (2007, 164).

---

10 Lorde recounts, by way of example, an experience with her daughter: "I watched while she worked it out bit by hurtful bit – what she really wanted – feeling her rage wax and wane, feeling her anger building against me because I could not help her do it nor do it for her, nor would she allow that" (2007, 158).

If, at times, anger seemed to keep her alive, "like guilt, [it was] an incomplete form of human knowledge" (2007, 152). It may clarify differences, especially in middle-depth relations like those in NWSA where connections were lacking, but the mode of strength it produces can demolish. As "a blind force . . . [it] cannot create the future" (Ibid.). It is retrospective, preoccupied with the hatred that birthed it. By contrast, even in a society "of entrenched loathing and contempt for whatever is Black and female . . . . Black women have a history of the use and sharing of power" (2007, 151).

Lorde concludes, "We will begin to see each other as we dare to begin to see ourselves; we will begin to see ourselves as we begin to see each other" (2007, 173). And as "we fear each other less and value each other more, we will come to value recognition within each other's eyes as well as within our own and seek a balance between these visions" (Ibid.).

The Politics of Hatred versus A Politics of Listening

In elaborating the many uses of anger, both at the NWSA conference in 1981 and later, Lorde needed a more agile and precise vocabulary. At its core was a distinction between anger and hatred, to which fury was also added.[11]

Lorde differentiated between the *ultimate aims* of anger (or rage) and of hatred. In "Eye to Eye," Lorde stated succinctly, "Anger [is] a passion of displeasure that may be excessive or misplaced but not necessarily harmful. Hatred [is] an emotional habit or attitude of mind in which aversion is coupled with ill will. Anger, used, does not destroy. Hatred does" (2007, 152). In "The Uses of Anger," she elaborates that anger furthers growth, survival, and learning, whereas "[h]atred is the fury of those who do not share our goals, and its object is death and destruction" (2007, 129).

---

11 To explain "fury," Lorde shifted from the distinction between a frustrated commitment to difference and a desire for its obliteration to a question of duration. "Anger is an appropriate reaction to racist attitudes, as is fury when the actions arising from those attitudes do not change" (2007, 129). Fury, then, is the response to inaction when what should be responded to already merited anger. And yet it remains. Fury also describes enduring repeated circumstances that would, in isolation, lead only to anger. Lorde writes: "There are so many occasions in each of our lives for righteous fury, multiplied and dividing" (2007, 160). She enumerates at being told Black women are somehow better, worse, never equal to Black men and other women and human beings. Fury can lead to the previously mentioned, all-too-common self-destruction of "fallen sisters." Still fury is not entirely unrelated to hatred: "Why do Black women reserve a particular voice of fury and disappointment for each other? . . . . This cruelty between us, this harshness, is a piece of the legacy of hate with which we were inoculated" (2007, 159).

Though anger expresses "the grief of distortions between peers" (Ibid.), it seeks growth through building alternative structures, horizons, and possibilities that hatred would seek only to crush. If anger expresses a desire to be in relation – even if much transformation is required for such connection to be possible – hatred is nihilistic, aiming to obliterate anything that embodies possibilities in the plural.[12] Anger, even when excessive or misplaced, insists on the value of difference, chafing in response to difference distorted, ready, if already with frustration, to fumble toward clarification. Hatred, on the other hand, works to naturalize, solidify, or even deepen inequalities. The only form of difference that those who promote hatred can abide is "sex difference" understood in binary terms within the structure of the nuclear family. In short, anger, *when used*, is a critical response to white supremacy's violent racism; hatred, by contrast, is its enabling vector.

But, as crucial as this distinction was for Lorde, most white feminists, some Black male leaders working for Black liberation, and many others often missed it. Their error was not difficult to understand. After all, Lorde describes hatred as suffusing U.S. popular culture, replete in newspapers, movies, comic books, and radio programs, evident in the gaze of the white world's mundane interactions with People of Color.[13]

Moreover, we miss it because the belief systems that structure our lives – coloniality, heteropatriarchy, racial capitalism, settler colonialism, and white supremacy – teach us first to fear difference and then to hate what we fear. This strategy, of obscuring the creative potential in our differences, makes coordinated responses to racist and other linked modes of oppression seem impossible. Such a strategy is painfully evident today, as right-wing extremism, and in some instances, outright fascism, promote hatred of non-European immigrants, sexually diverse people, ethnic and racialized minorities, religions, including Islam and Judaism, and all women who reject gender subordination. To these ascendant right-wing extremists, difference appears so existentially threatening, that it requires elimination, with a seeming delight in punitive cruelty.

12 When asking whether Black women might be less inclined to crucify each other if they had "been allowed Black goddesses, Black heroines . . . our mothers and our selves in their/our own magnificence," (2007, 165) Lorde frames a function of hatred as obfuscating "the beauty which is power in ourselves" (Ibid.).

13 Lorde writes, "my wished-for death, seen in the eyes of so many white people from the time I could see" (2007, 147).

Lorde authored her poignant reflections at UCONN in a similar political moment. She therefore clarifies, in part in response to frustration from members at the NWSA conference who thought women needed to close ranks in response to the rise of the so-called New Right and the Moral Majority, that she was aiming to do just that. Lorde wrote:

> So we are working in a context of opposition and threat, the cause of which is certainly not the angers which lie between us, but rather that virulent hatred leveled against all women, people of Color, lesbians and gay men, poor people – against all of us who are seeking to examine the particulars of our lives as we resist our oppressions, moving toward coalition and effective action. (2007, 128)

Lorde clarified that frustrations, and even profound senses of betrayal, among women were still caused by people of common cause. They might disagree, sometimes bitterly, about how best to fight their oppression. But it was dangerous to mistake this internal exasperation and alienation for the destructive hatred of people, then steadily growing in organization and potential power.

She added, "we must be quite serious about the choice of this topic [of women fighting racism] . . . because, rest assured, our opponents are quite serious about their hatred of us and of what we are trying to do here" (2007, 128-9). To illustrate, she reminded listeners that it was not *their* anger that gave her reason to caution them to lock their doors or not wander the Hartford streets alone. "It is the hatred which lurks in those streets, that urge to destroy us all if we truly work for change" (2007, 129). Put simply, it was not the anger of any women, certainly not Black women, that was enacting a "dehumanizing power, bent upon the annihilation of us all" (2007, 133). Instead, dehumanization is the result of racist hatred.

Lorde's poetry, social theory, editorial work, pedagogy, and grassroots activism sought to undermine the fear of difference, particularly as it manifested in terms of race, gender, and sexuality. These different roles she played throughout her life revealed her commitment to ending the oppressions of those who were most vulnerable. Perhaps unsurprisingly, Lorde's personal, professional, and activist trajectory enacted the lesson that anger is transformed into change through action, which often took the form of meaningful everyday interventions in those spaces where one can exert influence.

Her life's work demonstrates that critical analysis pursued through the rigorous scrutiny of anger could be powerfully illuminating, revealing the kinds of praxis worthy of engagement. Thus, for Lorde, critical reflection was necessary but insufficient. Radical transformation depended on valuing devalued forms of knowing, including the information and questions revealed in affective registers we were taught to hide and disdain. But such valuing rarely emerged absent deliberate everyday coalition-nurturing between Women of Color and white women committed to self and collective transformation.

While such work was onerous, it was also punctuated by unforgettable moments of joy. One source of joy, Lorde powerfully suggested, could come from learning to "mother ourselves" in the face of unremitting hatred, violence, and destruction (2007, 173). Such mothering, for Lorde, entailed:

> [E]stablish[ing] authority over our own definition[s], provid[ing] an attentive concern and expectation of growth which is the beginning of that acceptance we came to expect only from our mothers. It means... affirm[ing] my own worth by committing myself to my own survival, in my own self and in the self of other Black women. On the other hand, it means that as I learn my worth and genuine possibility, I refuse to settle for anything less than a rigorous pursuit of the possible in myself, at the same time making a distinction between what is possible and what the outside world drives me to do to prove I am human. It means being able to recognize my successes, and to be tender with myself, even when I fail. (Ibid.)

"Mothering ourselves," for Lorde, meant countering racist hatred by cultivating radical love in relationship to ourselves, our histories, and our endeavors. It means refusing the model of fearful, difference-loathing creatures as *who we must be*. Central to such love is the exact opposite of the presently widening ethnic, geopolitical, legal, and religious cleavages we are urged to normalize through our support. Radical love is the "unromantic and tedious work" (2007, 142) of navigating merited distrust, misunderstanding, and frustration to see the world-transforming and potential creative beauty when and where our differences meet. Crucial to doing so is remaining committed in the absence of any assurance that whatever we seek will immediately or ever "work" (2007, 142).

One expression of radical love is a *politics of listening*. Briefly delineated in "The Uses of Anger," combating cooptation, defensiveness, exclusion, and misnaming, active, careful listening can promote mutual understanding. Beyond the perils of sterile guilt or distancing evasion, we can lay down our arms and open ourselves, inviting in the language and claims of others with humility and with love.[14]

Lorde warns that the politics of listening is not easy. First, we must listen with at least the intensity with which we are inclined to defend ourselves. As noted, Lorde acknowledges it is "very difficult to stand still and to listen to another woman's voice" as she lays out a grievance not familiar to Lorde, or worse, created by her, own actions (2007, 128). Yet, if we care sufficiently to slow down and to learn from those we hurt by our actions (or inactions), the relations that emerge can be unprecedented. If we can *turn toward* anger, we can turn toward insight and away from the "deadly, and safely familiar" (2007, 131). A politics of listening can foster the kind of human ties that can begin to dismantle multifaceted conditions of unfreedom, enabling us to fathom and digest who profits from the hatreds expressed in heterosexism, patriarchy, and racial capitalism.[15] Lorde insisted, "we still know that the power to kill is less than the power to create, for it produces an ending rather than the beginning of something new" (2007, 152).

For all the reasons explored here, Lorde saw the struggle against racism, which demanded a historically feminized mode of listening, as necessarily feminist (Abod 2002). Yet, as we have shown, she did not treat feminism uncritically. On the contrary, a genuine feminism, one with a demonstrated commitment not only to the flourishing of all women, but to recognition that the category "woman" is itself ever expanding, demanded a capacity – yet to emerge – for listening attentively to one's own and other women's anger.

---

14 For Lorde, the erotic over- or undertones here were intentional. For more, see her "Uses of the Erotic" in the same volume.

15 Indeed, Lorde wrote that Black women and white women facing each other as genuine peers was itself "heretical and generative" (2007, 129).

Still, in "The Transformation of Silence into Language and Action," Lorde roots our individual and collective possibility in an honest assessment of who we are:

> We can learn to work and speak when we are afraid in the same way we have learned to work and speak when we are tired. For we have been socialized to respect fear more than our own needs for language and definition, and while we wait in silence for that final luxury of fearlessness, the weight of that silence will choke us. (2007, 44)

In marking fifty years of WGSS at UCONN, we are seeking above our many legitimate fears to advance our shared need for language, definition, listening, and *actually meeting* in and through our differences. We see both feminism and a future as depending on it.

Works Cited

Abod, Jennifer, and Audre Lorde. *The Edge of Each Other's Battles*. Women Make Movies, 2022.

Cep, Cassey. "The Perils and Possibilities of Anger: After centuries of censure, women reconsider the political power of female rage." *The New Yorker Magazine*. October 8, 2018. https://www.newyorker.com/magazine/2018/10/15/the- perils-and-possibilities-of-anger

Cooper, Anna Julia. *The Voice of Anna Julia Cooper: Including A Voice from the South and Other Important Essays, Papers, and Letters* (Legacies of Social Thought Series), edited by Charles Lemert and Esme Bhan. Rowman and Littlefield, 1998.

Cooper, Brittney. *Eloquent Rage: A Black Feminist Discovers Her Superpower*. St. Martin's Press, 2018.

Lee, Robert, Tristan Ahtone, Margaret Pearce, Kalen Goodluck, Geoff McGhee, Cody Leff, Katherine Lanpher, and Taryn Salinas. "Land-Grab Universities: A *High Country News* Investigation." https://www.landgrabu.org, 2021.

Aimee. "History of the Women's Studies to Women's, Gender, and Sexuality Studies Program." Unpublished student paper, University of Connecticut, 2017-2018.

Lorde, Audre. "Power." In *The Collected Poems of Audre Lorde*. W. W. Norton and Company Inc., 1997. Pp. 319–320.

Lorde, Audre. "The Transformation of Silence into Language and Action." In *Sister Outsider: Essays and Speeches*. Crossing Over Press, [1984] 2007. Pp. 40-44.

Lorde, Audre. "The Master's Tools Will Never Dismantle the Master's House." In *Sister Outsider: Essays and Speeches*. Crossing Over Press, [1984] 2007. Pp. 110-113.

Lorde, Audre. "The Uses of Anger: Women Responding to Racism." In *Sister Outsider: Essays and Speeches*. Crossing Over Press, [1984] 2007. Pp. 124-133.

Lorde, Audre. "Learning from the 60s." In *Sister Outsider: Essays and Speeches*. Crossing Over Press, [1984] 2007. Pp. 134-144.

Lorde, Audre. "Eye to Eye: Black Women, Hatred, and Anger." In *Sister Outsider: Essays and Speeches*. Crossing Over Press, [1984] 2007. Pp. 145-175.

Ross, Loretta J. "The Origin of the Phrase 'Women of Color.'" *YouTube*, Western States Center, 15 Feb. 2011, www.youtube.com/watch?v=82vl34mi4Iw.

The Uses of Anger: Women Responding to Racism

Audre Lorde[1]

Racism. The belief in the inherent superiority of one race over all others and thereby the right to dominance, manifest and implied.

Women respond to racism. My response to racism is anger. I have lived with that anger, ignoring it, feeding upon it, learning to use it before it laid my visions to waste, for most of my life. Once I did it in silence, afraid of the weight. My fear of anger taught me nothing. Your fear of that anger will teach you nothing, also.

Women responding to racism means women responding to anger; the anger of exclusion, of unquestioned privilege, of racial distortions, of silence, ill-use, stereotyping, defensiveness, misnaming, betrayal, and co-optation.

My anger is a response to racist attitudes and to the actions and presumptions that arise out of those attitudes. If your dealings with other women reflect those attitudes, then my anger and your attendant fears are spotlights that can be used for growth in the same way I have used learning to express anger for my growth. But for corrective surgery, not guilt. Guilt and defensiveness are bricks in a wall against which we all flounder; they serve none of our futures.

Because I do not want this to become a theoretical discussion, I am going to give a few examples of interchanges between women that illustrate these points. In the interest of time, I am going to cut them short. I want you to know there were many more.

---

1 Keynote presentation at the National Women's Studies Association (NWSA) Conference, Storrs, Connecticut, June 1981.

For example:

- I speak out of direct and particular anger at an academic conference, and a white woman says, "Tell me how you feel but don't say it too harshly or I cannot hear you." But is it my manner that keeps her from hearing, or the threat of a message that her life may change?
- The Women's Studies Program of a southern university invites a Black woman to read following a week-long forum on Black and white women. "What has this week given to you?" I ask. The most vocal white woman says, "I think I've gotten a lot. I feel Black women really understand me a lot better now; they have a better idea of where I'm coming from." As if understanding her lay at the core of the racist problem.
- After fifteen years of a women's movement which professes to address the life concerns and possible futures of all women, I still hear, on campus after campus, "How can we address the issues of racism? No women of Color attended." Or, the other side of that statement: "We have no one in our department equipped to teach their work." In other words, racism is a Black women's problem, a problem of women of Color, and only we can discuss it.
- After I read from my work entitled "Poems for Women in Rage,"[2] a white woman asks me: "Are you going to do anything with how we can deal directly with *our* anger? I feel it's so important." I ask, "How do you use *your* rage?" And then I have to turn away from the blank look in her eyes, before she can invite me to participate in her own annihilation. I do not exist to feel her anger for her.
- White women are beginning to examine their relationships to Black women, yet often I hear them wanting only to deal with little colored children across the roads of childhood, the beloved nursemaid, the occasional second-grade classmate – those tender memories of what was mysterious and intriguing or neutral. You avoid the childhood assumptions formed by the raucous laughter at Rastus and Alfalfa, the acute message of your mommy's handkerchief spread upon

---

2 One poem from this series is included in *Chosen Poems: Old and New* (W.W. Norton and Company, New York, 1978), pp. 105–108.

the park bench because I had just been sitting there, the indelible and dehumanizing portraits of Amos 'n Andy and your daddy's humorous bedtime stories.[3]

- I wheel my two-year-old daughter in a shopping cart through a supermarket in Eastchester in 1967, and a little white girl riding past in her mother's cart calls out excitedly, "Oh look, Mommy, a baby maid!" And your mother shushes you, but she does not correct you. And so fifteen years later, at a conference on racism, you can still find that story humorous. But I hear your laughter is full of terror and dis-ease.

- A white academic welcomes the appearance of a collection of non-Black women of color.[4] "It allows me to deal with racism without dealing with the harshness of Black women," she says to me.

- At an international cultural gathering of women, a well-known white american poet interrupts the reading of the work of women of Color to read her own poem, and then dashes off to an "important panel."

If women in the academy truly want a dialogue about racism, it will require recognizing the needs and the living contexts of other women. When an academic woman says, "I can't afford it," she may mean she is making a choice about how to spend her available money. But when a woman on welfare says, "I can't afford it," she means she is surviving on an amount of money that was barely subsistence in 1972, and she often does not have enough to eat. Yet the National Women's Studies Association here in 1981 holds a conference in which it commits itself to responding to racism, yet refuses to waive the registration fee for poor women and women of Color who wished to present and conduct workshops. This has

---

[3] Editors' Note: Joel Chandler Harris introduced "Rastus" as a derogatory Black male character with Black deacon, "Brer Rastus," in his first *Uncle Remus* book in 1880. A shortening of the Greek name "Erastus," as in Erastus of Corinth, Rastus figures were simple Black males happy with their subordinate racialized status. Recycled in minstrel shows, radio, and popular songs, Rastus was also the name of the jolly Black chef character on Cream of Wheat cereal boxes beginning in 1893. Selling nostalgia for a past when racial hierarchies were thought to have been unquestionably embraced, the image was central to the wildly successful sales of this product. Similarly, a national U.S. craze and radio institution, *The Amos 'n Andy Show*, was broadcast nightly from coast to coast in the 1930s and 40s. Created, written, and voiced by two white U.S. actors who played Amos Jones and Andrew Brown, they drew from minstrel traditions, including caricatured Black dialect, intonation, and character traits. In response to protests by the National Association for the Advancement of Colored People (NAACP), the television show, which began airing in 1951, was canceled in 1954, although it remained in syndication until 1966.

[4] *This Bridge Called My Back: Writings by Radical Women of Color* edited by Cherríe Moraga and Gloria Anzaldúa (Kitchen Table: Women of Color Press, New York, 1984), first published in 1981.

made it impossible for many women of Color – for instance, Wilmette Brown, of Black Women for Wages for Housework – to participate in this conference. Is this to be merely another case of the academy discussing life within the closed circuits of the academy?

To the white women present who recognize these attitudes as familiar, but most of all, to all my sisters of Color who live and survive thousands of such encounters – to my sisters of Color who like me still tremble their rage under harness, or who sometimes question the expression of our rage as useless and disruptive (the two most popular accusations) – I want to speak about anger, my anger, and what I have learned from my travels through its dominions.

Everything can be used/except what is wasteful/(you will need/to remember this when you are accused of destruction.)[5]

Every woman has a well-stocked arsenal of anger potentially useful against those oppressions, personal and institutional, which brought that anger into being. Focused with precision it can become a powerful source of energy serving progress and change. And when I speak of change, I do not mean a simple switch of positions or a temporary lessening of tensions, nor the ability to smile or feel good. I am speaking of a basic and radical alteration in those assumptions underlining our lives.

I have seen situations where white women hear a racist remark, resent what has been said, become filled with fury, and remain silent because they are afraid. That unexpressed anger lies within them like an undetonated device, usually to be hurled at the first woman of Color who talks about racism.

But anger expressed and translated into action in the service of our vision and our future is a liberating and strengthening act of clarification, for it is in the painful process of this translation that we identify who are our allies with whom we have grave differences, and who are our genuine enemies.

Anger is loaded with information and energy. When I speak of women of Color, I do not only mean Black women. The woman of Color who is not Black and who charges me with rendering her invisible

---

5 From "For Each of You," first published in *From A Land Where Other People Live* (Broadside Press, Detroit, 1973), and collected in *Chosen Poems: Old and New* (W.W. Norton and Company, New York, 1982), p. 42.

by assuming that her struggles with racism are identical with my own has something to tell me that I had better learn from, lest we both waste ourselves fighting the truths between us. If I participate, knowingly or otherwise, in my sister's oppression and she calls me on it, to answer her anger with my own only blankets the substance of our exchange with reaction. It wastes energy. And yes, it is very difficult to stand still and to listen to another woman's voice delineate an agony I do not share, or one to which I myself have contributed.

In this place we speak removed from the more blatant reminders of our embattlement as women. This need not blind us to the size and complexities of the forces mounting against us and all that is most human within our environment. We are not here as women examining racism in a political and social vacuum. We operate in the teeth of a system for which racism and sexism are primary, established, and necessary props of profit. Women responding to racism is a topic so dangerous that when the local media attempt to discredit this conference they choose to focus upon the provision of lesbian housing as a diversionary device – as if the Hartford *Courant* dare not mention the topic chosen for discussion here, racism, lest it become apparent that women are in fact attempting to examine and to alter all the repressive conditions of our lives.

Mainstream communication does not want women, particularly white women, responding to racism. It wants racism to be accepted as an immutable given in the fabric of your existence, like evening time or the common cold.

So we are working in a context of opposition and threat, the cause of which is certainly not the angers which lie between us, but rather that virulent hatred leveled against all women, people of Color, lesbians and gay men, poor people – against all of us who are seeking to examine the particulars of our lives as we resist our oppressions, moving toward coalition and effective action.

Any discussion among women about racism must include the recognition and the use of anger. This discussion must be direct and creative because it is crucial. We cannot allow our fear of anger to deflect us nor seduce us into settling for anything less than the hard work of excavating honesty; we must be quite serious about the choice of this topic and the angers entwined within it because, rest assured, our opponents are quite serious about their hatred of us and of what we are trying to do here.

And while we scrutinize the often painful face of each other's anger, please remember that it is not our anger which makes me caution you to lock your doors at night and not to wander the streets of Hartford alone. It is the hatred which lurks in those streets, the urge to destroy us all if we truly work for change rather than merely indulge in academic rhetoric.

This hatred and our anger are very different. Hatred is the fury of those who do not share our goals, and its object is death and destruction. Anger is a grief of distortions between peers, and its object is change. But our time is getting shorter. We have been raised to view any difference other than sex as a reason for destruction, and for Black women and white women to face each other's angers without denial or immobility or silence or guilt is in itself a heretical and generative idea. It implies peers meeting upon a common basis to examine difference, and to alter those distortions which history has created around our difference. For it is those distortions which separate us. And we must ask ourselves: Who profits from all this?

Women of Color in America have grown up within a symphony of anger, at being silenced, at being unchosen, at knowing that when we survive, it is in spite of a world that takes for granted our lack of humanness, and which hates our very existence outside of its service. And I say *symphony* rather than *cacophony* because we have had to learn to orchestrate those furies so that they do not tear us apart. We have had to learn to move through them and use them for strength and force and insight within our daily lives. Those of us who did not learn this difficult lesson did not survive. And part of my anger is always libation for my fallen sisters.

Anger is an appropriate reaction to racist attitudes, as is fury when the actions arising from those attitudes do not change. To those women here who fear the anger of women of Color more than their own unscrutinized racist attitudes, I ask: Is the anger of women of Color more threatening than the woman-hatred that tinges all aspects of our lives?

It is not the anger of other women that will destroy us but our refusals to stand still, to listen to its rhythms, to learn within it, to move beyond the manner of presentation to the substance, to tap that anger as an important source of empowerment.

I cannot hide my anger to spare your guilt, nor hurt feelings, nor answering anger; for to do so insults and trivializes all our efforts. Guilt is not a response to anger; it is a response to one's own actions or lack of action. If it leads to change then it can be useful, since it is then no longer guilt but the beginning of knowledge. Yet all too often, guilt is just another name for impotence, for defensiveness destructive of communication; it becomes a device to protect ignorance and the continuation of things the way they are, the ultimate protection for changelessness.

Most women have not developed tools for facing anger constructively. CR groups in the past, largely white, dealt with how to express anger, usually at the world of men.[6] And these groups were made up of white women who shared the terms of their oppressions. There was usually little attempt to articulate the genuine differences between women, such as those of race, color, age, class, and sexual identity. There was no apparent need at that time to examine the contradictions of self, woman as oppressor. There was work on expressing anger, but very little on anger directed against each other. No tools were developed to deal with other women's anger except to avoid it, deflect it, or flee from it under a blanket of guilt.

I have no creative use for guilt, yours or my own. Guilt is only another way of avoiding informed action, of buying time out of the pressing need to make clear choices, out of the approaching storm that can feed the earth as well as bend the trees. If I speak to you in anger, at least I have spoken to you: I have not put a gun to your head and shot you down in the street; I have not looked at your bleeding sister's body and asked, "What did she do to deserve it?" This was the reaction of two white women to Mary Church Terrell's telling of the lynching of a pregnant Black woman whose baby was then torn from her body. That was in 1921, and Alice Paul had just refused to publicly endorse the enforcement of the Nineteenth Amendment for all women – by refusing to endorse the inclusion of women of Color, although we had worked to help bring about that amendment.

The angers between women will not kill us if we can articulate them with precision, if we listen to the content of what is said with at least as much intensity as we defend ourselves against the manner of saying.

---

6 Editors' Note: "CR" referred to consciousness-raising groups.

When we turn from anger we turn from insight, saying we will accept only the designs already known, deadly and safely familiar. I have tried to learn my anger's usefulness to me, as well as its limitations.

For women raised to fear, too often anger threatens annihilation. In the male construct of brute force, we were taught that our lives depended upon the good will of patriarchal power. The anger of others was to be avoided at all costs because there was nothing to be learned from it but pain, a judgment that we had been bad girls, come up lacking, not done what we were supposed to do. And if we accept our powerlessness, then of course any anger can destroy us.

But the strength of women lies in recognizing differences between us as creative, and in standing to those distortions which we inherited without blame, but which are now ours to alter. The angers of women can transform difference through insight into power. For anger between peers births change, not destruction, and the discomfort and sense of loss it often causes is not fatal, but a sign of growth.

My response to racism is anger. That anger has eaten clefts into my living only when it remained unspoken, useless to anyone. It has also served me in classrooms without light or learning, where the work and history of Black women was less than a vapor. It has served me as fire in the ice zone of uncomprehending eyes of white women who see in my experience and the experience of my people only new reasons for fear or guilt. And my anger is no excuse for not dealing with your blindness, no reason to withdraw from the results of your own actions.

When women of Color speak out of the anger that laces so many of our contacts with white women, we are often told that we are "creating a mood of hopelessness," "preventing white women from getting past guilt," or "standing in the way of trusting communication and action." All these quotes come directly from letters to me from members of this organization within the last two years. One woman wrote, "Because you are Black and Lesbian, you seem to speak with the moral authority of suffering." Yes, I am Black and Lesbian, and what you hear in my voice is fury, not suffering. Anger, not moral authority. There is a difference.

To turn aside from the anger of Black women with excuses or the pretexts of intimidation is to award no one power – it is merely another way of preserving racial blindness, the power of unaddressed privilege, unbreached, intact. Guilt is only another form of objectification. Oppressed peoples are always being asked to stretch a little more, to bridge the gap between blindness and humanity. Black women are expected to use our anger only in the service of other people's salvation or learning. But that time is over. My anger has meant pain to me but it has also meant survival, and before I give it up I'm going to be sure that there is something at least as powerful to replace it on the road to clarity.

What woman here is so enamored of her own oppression that she cannot see her heelprint upon another woman's face? What woman's terms of oppression have become precious and necessary to her as a ticket into the fold of the righteous, away from the cold winds of self-scrutiny?

I am a lesbian woman of Color whose children eat regularly because I work in a university. If their full bellies make me fail to recognize my commonality with a woman of Color whose children do not eat because she cannot find work, or who has no children because her insides are rotted from home abortions and sterilization; if I fail to recognize the lesbian who chooses not to have children, the woman who remains closeted because her homophobic community is her only life support, the woman who chooses silence instead of another death, the woman who is terrified lest my anger trigger the explosion of hers; if I fail to recognize them as other faces of myself, then I am contributing not only to each of their oppressions but also to my own, and the anger which stands between us then must be used for clarity and mutual empowerment, not for evasion by guilt or for further separation. I am not free while any woman is unfree, even when her shackles are very different from my own. And I am not free as long as one person of Color remains chained. Nor is any one of you.

I speak here as a woman of Color who is not bent upon destruction, but upon survival. No woman is responsible for altering the psyche of her oppressor, even when that psyche is embodied in another woman. I have suckled the wolf's lip of anger and I have used it for illumination, laughter, protection, fire in places where there was no light, no food, no sisters, no quarter. We are not goddesses or matriarchs or edifices of divine forgiveness; we are not fiery fingers of judgment or instruments of flagellation;

we are women forced back always upon our woman's power. We have learned to use anger as we have learned to use the dead flesh of animals, and bruised, battered, and changing, we have survived and grown and, in Angela Wilson's words, we *are* moving on. With or without uncolored women. We use whatever strengths we have fought for, including anger, to help define and fashion a world where all our sisters can grow, where our children can love, and where the power of touching and meeting another woman's difference and wonder will eventually transcend the need for destruction.

For it is not the anger of Black women which is dripping down over this globe like a diseased liquid. It is not my anger that launches rockets, spends over sixty thousand dollars a second on missiles and other agents of war and death, slaughters children in cities, stockpiles nerve gas and chemical bombs, sodomizes our daughters and our earth. It is not the anger of Black women which corrodes into blind, dehumanizing power, bent upon the annihilation of us all unless we meet it with what we have, our power to examine and to redefine the terms upon which we will live and work; our power to envision and to reconstruct, anger by painful anger, stone upon heavy stone, a future of pollinating difference and the earth to support our choices.

We welcome all women who can meet us, face to face, beyond objectification and beyond guilt.

To Grow Through Genealogy: An Interview with M. Jacqui Alexander and Beverly Guy-Sheftall

Briona Simone Jones

Briona Simone Jones (BSJ): I want to begin by talking about your choice to build Women's Studies. You both have built Women's Studies in different ways at different institutions and even in your larger communities.

M. Jacqui Alexander (MJA): I thought a lot about this, and about the questions you sent for us. And one of the things that occurred to me about our choices to build Women's Studies is that it's not only Women Studies. The vision, the vision for freedom, freedom for women of all kinds across the globe has intersected with other kinds of freedoms. It's intersected with our colonial struggle, coming from the Caribbean primarily.

I remember my first conference, hearing questions of violence against women when I was in Jamaica, which raises this question of the violence in the home melding with state violence – that the state patriarch and the private patriarch will be almost one in the same. And so, they gave us a new way to think about violence against women.

And then, all through the eighties, there was this incredible blossoming of Women of Color politics in response to some serious violence. In 1979, there were the Roxbury murders in Boston, and we have Combahee and the starting of Kitchen Table: Women of Color Press. So, there are genealogies of Women's Studies and those genealogies don't necessarily always start in the U.S. That's important to say: *they don't always start in the U.S.* They start in an elsewhere.

That gives us a hook to think about how it is that Audre herself, her own work, ended up being transnational, with meetings and movements in Amsterdam, in South Africa, in Germany. In particular, Sisterhood in Support of Sisters in South Africa. It was always a transnational endeavor and that's how I came to be.

In coming out as lesbian, I was also coming out as an immigrant Woman of Color in the U.S. – those two things were simultaneous. The building of Women's Studies, then, has grown out of that genealogy, that history. Most of the work in Women's Studies, the work that Beverly and I did at Spelman [College] was linking Women's Studies to Sexuality Studies because so often they are not tethered when they very much need to be tethered to one another.

Beverly Guy-Sheftall (BGS): I'm going to echo Jacqui and start with her first point. For me, Women's Studies and my interest, my passion for Women's Studies came initially from my involvement in the Civil Rights Movement – growing up in the Jim and Jane Crow South of Memphis and being in Atlanta with the Atlanta student movement. And being very conscious of what was going on with SNCC [the Student Nonviolent Coordinating Committee] and with people like Frances Beale, who had initially been in Paris. And so, for me, it was located in Black Liberation, though we had to critique the patriarchal and heterosexist aspects of it. But it came from growing up in the South, being in the student movement, being very aware of SNCC and it's transnational, radical critique of the problems of the Civil Rights Movement, such as it being male-dominated. They also had a critique of the Women's Movement.

I just want to mention, in this regard, because it echoes again what Jacqui said. SNCC people have always had something to say about Palestine. Radical Black women were always thinking about the world. I'm thinking about Toni Cade Bambara. When I interviewed her three years after the *Black Woman* came out, one of the things she warned us about was U.S. Black Feminists not being transnational enough and not being in solidarity, for example, with Latina women and women all over the world, particularly women of the Global South.

I always thought of Women's Studies and the Women's Movement as a global, radical movement that did not need to be narrowly focused on the U.S., and certainly being connected to liberation struggles that may not have a gender or sexuality focus.

MJA: Yeah, it's important to make the point about Palestine early instead of at the end. I remember when Audre [Lorde] received the honorary degree at Oberlin [College]. The backlash was absolutely fierce.

Or June Jordan. We can make a list of people for whom thinking about the social, political, economic, and cultural conditions of people in various places – thinking that way gives us the best lens to understand the "local" which is always already transnational. There is no local that exists by itself. So thinking about that together with thinking about solidarity. It's not just a question of analyses – of being theoretical and making divisions. It's really more about how do you build solidarity? And what are those politics anchored upon? What are they linked to? And who are you linked with? Who are you in conversation with?

BGS: I was in the audience at the NWSA conference [in 1981 in Storrs, Connecticut] when Audre delivered that piece. She set that place on fire. It's hard to imagine, first of all, how courageous and in your face and explicit and clear she was about racism. Racism abroad, but certainly racism within the Women's Movement. It was amazing to be in that audience. I think my mouth was open!

That was one of the most important moments in my journey in Women's Studies, the Women's Movement, and Women of Color radical politics. It had a huge impact on me politically. The moment symbolized that you have to open your mouth and be clear and explicit. Even if you are upsetting people. Some of the People of Color in the audience were not so happy.

BSJ: You met bell hooks at this particular National Women's Studies Association conference?

BGS: Yes, I met bell hooks at that conference. I did not know her yet. She was promoting her book. She didn't have anywhere to stay. She had no resources. I asked her to come and stay with me. I slept on the floor. We were in the dorm, and she had my little single bed and we started talking that night and continued to talk up until the week before she died.

MJA: That's such a crucial point: friendships get formed in the process of political struggle.

BGS: Yes!

MJA: Like, for life. I recall that Barbara Smith had convened a Woman of Color Institute for radical research and action. She convened a bunch of us. Chandra [Talpade Mohanty] was in that group. That's where I met Chandra for the first time, Alia Arasoughly, the Palestinian filmmaker, and Gloria Joseph were in that group. We stayed friends for life. In doing the work, you cultivate the friendships. Those never change, right? Political projects and situations might change, the urgency of the political project does not change.

BGS: Let me say something in that regard about what I share with my students about my political sister friends. I came into Audre's orbit because of her friendship with Johnnetta Cole. Of course I knew who Audre was, but their close friendship enabled us, for example, to get the Audre Lorde Papers to the Spelman Archive. Johnnetta was already friends with Gloria Joseph, which helped us acquire her papers, too. So, the friendship between Johnetta, Audre, Gloria, and Spelman, emerge for precisely the reason you just mentioned, Jacqui.

MJA: Yeah.

BGS: *I Am Your Sister*, the book I co-edited with Rudolph P. Byrd and Johnnetta B. Cole, included unpublished writings that were in the archives here at Spelman.

BSJ: Why invoke Audre Lorde's work at this particular historical moment?

MJA: It can never be through this trajectory of feminism alone. There is nothing in Audre's work that is that single-focused. We have a history of all kinds of analyses, of The Combahee River Collective, intersectionality, the simultaneity of oppression, transnationality. You can call it whatever you want. Once it encompasses this idea that ultimately everything belongs to everything else – it's all interrelated and it's that interrelatedness of structures and people that we want to bring home to students in particular. Look at the onslaught now of identifying and pushing people further into silos.

BGS: Yeah.

MJA: So how will we offset that? How do we build our solidarity movements to offset something so huge?

BGS: I noticed, and other people notice, that, in terms of book bans, many of the [banned] books were Black Feminist texts. I would argue that in many ways it's because they've been the most critical, the most radical, the most intersectional, the most hard-hitting. These texts were on the banned books list more than generic Black books.

MJA: Yeah. And let's continue to use that word *radical*.

BGS: Yes! We have to resuscitate that word.

BSJ: Why are there so many chasms in Women's Studies and Gender and Sexuality Studies pertaining to solidarity and transnational coalition-building? I'm thinking about what's happening globally right now in Sudan, the Congo, Ghana, Palestine, and Atlanta.

BGS: I'll share something I recall bell hooks saying a decade ago. She said Women's, Gender, and Sexuality Studies, which was not called that then, had become institutionalized in the academy, and had lost its radical edge. It almost forgot that its mission is also being connected to an outside world and to activist projects, which is how Women's Studies started. Women's Studies comes out of Women's movements. Black Studies comes out of the Civil Rights Movement. And bell hooks would say: Women's Studies is becoming like the regular disciplines. Professors are coming in and focusing on their tenure promotion, and being told in many ways that they can't get involved in all that other stuff. You know, you have to get tenure.

And, generally speaking, Women's, Gender, and Sexuality Studies has been fairly U.S.-focused, so Palestine would be way out of the lens of most Women's, Gender, and Sexuality programs. And of course, now it's dangerous.

MJA: Yeah.

BGS: The Women's, Gender, and Sexuality Studies Department at Barnard is where Premilla Nadasen is now under attack. They are under attack, and have been moved to actually fire chairs in Women's, Gender, and Sexuality Studies who say anything about Palestine.

MJA: What that requires, then, is building solidarity amongst the knowledge elements, the theoretical elements on the campus. When Chandra and I did this article looking at a number of Women's Studies programs throughout the country, we found some really important, disturbing elements. One is of that separation between the academy and community that perhaps continues up until now.

BGS: Yeah.

BSJ: Yeah.

MJA: The second was that there is a lot of latent colonialism in knowledges that are supposed to be radical. I found it when I was doing work looking at white gay tourism. Those advertising gestures to encourage folks to "come to the third world." All of those gestures resembled colonial travel narratives. There is a strong colonial impulse still operating in this world.

BGS: Yeah.

MJA: The third thing Chandra and I found was that most often students were ahead of their teachers. Students were the ones who were involved in activism and raising questions which departments were reluctant to take up. Students are carrying the banner while the professors are more reluctant to take up these questions.

And then there is professionalization within the discipline, precisely what Beverly was talking about. Professionalization.

BGS: Yeah.

MJA: Now you believe you have to protect tenure. Before you believed you had to protect yourself to get it. When you do get it, you believe that you have to protect yourself in order to keep it.

BGS: Exactly.

MJA: There are clearly larger structural forces at work, determining what happens within "programs" and "departments." I mean, how many years later? Fifty years later and we are still talking about the program.

BGS: Yeah.

BSJ: What do you think is the importance of invoking Audre's name or this particular essay in this moment?

BGS: I sometimes ask my students, *what makes you angry? And what do you like doing more than anything else?* The anger question is very difficult. I ask them, *what are you willing to die for?* And I get a blank answer. The next time I teach this essay ["The Uses of Anger"] by Lorde, I'm going to ask them those questions again. *What makes you angry?* My guess is that it won't be anything very political for most of them.

MJA: Hmm.

BGS: I mean, what makes this generation of Women of Color angry?

MJA: Yeah.

BGS: So that's a good question.

MJA: Why do we need to invoke Audre? She's no longer in the flesh. So, what does Audre's spirit still have to say to us? You can imagine that she still has a lot to say! To me, it's a question of expansiveness. Expansiveness because if we go back to that essay, it reminds me a little of the "Uses of the Erotic." It's a very economical essay. Five pages. Beverly, you heard the impact of that. You felt the impact of those five pages. The amount of ground that gets covered in five pages is absolutely phenomenal.

She gives us a distinction between fury and anger. She talked about anger's episteme, but she talks also about anger as providing important information. In other words, it's not a useless emotion. She has no patience for useless emotions like guilt. Like, *don't come close to her with guilt* because it's a useless emotion. And so, there's a deep understanding of Audre about this word, "anger," that is filled with energy.

There's this sentence: *if you don't use your power, it will be used against you.* That sense that things are energetic in the word. And so you want to tap into that energy for your sense of self. If you remember, she doesn't stop at anger. If we look at the broader Audre, she's not stopping at anger. She's also talking about joy. She is also talking about the erotic. And this is a piece about anger in relationship to racism. Remember, she also did "Eye to Eye: Black Women, Hatred, and Anger." I remember her saying that she gained 30-something pounds writing that essay! So, there are costs to this. There are real costs. There were real costs for her. And she always remembered those who did not make it.

So, to me, in invoking Audre, we must ask this question: *Who are we leaving behind? What are the blind spots in our own analyses that prevent us from doing radical work at this moment?* Things go underground at some historical moments. There are lots of earlier historical moments where people were forced underground.

BGS: Yeah.

MJA: We have the model and motto: The Underground Railroad. Underground. We may not always have to be visible in the ways we were in the 1960s and '70s.

BGS: I'm reminded, Jacqui, and this may seem oxymoronic, but reading that essay and seeing her, you really feel that there's joy in struggle.

MJA: Yeah.

BGS: Audre was not looking sad or beat down. She had a smile. She was exhilarated because of that energy and struggle. Struggle is not supposed to beat you down. It's daily and it's supposed to remind you of why you are on this earth. Struggle is not depressing. I mean, it doesn't have to be depressing.

MJA: Yeah. So, we get replenished.

BGS: Yes! Yes.

MJA: We get replenished when we are together. And yet there is also work that we have to do individually.

BGS: Yeah.

MJA: Your individual internal work that you constantly have to do in whatever form or shape you choose. But we get replenished.

So, the lessons are unfinished. I don't feel that within Women's Studies we have done enough with the work of Audre Lorde, Gloria Anzaldúa, or June Jordan. We haven't done enough. There is more left to do, as well there should be.

BSJ: How did "The Uses of Anger" shape your personal and political lives?

MJA: I met Audre during my first teaching appointment at Brandeis University in 1986. I had just gotten there, and people thought that I knew her. But I didn't. But that didn't prevent me from picking up the phone and calling her. The other reason that I called her was that I was living in Cambridge at the time with my partner, Jinny Chalmers, who was a white woman and very close friends with Angela Bowen, whose partner was also white. There was this huge issue. We couldn't do it. We just couldn't get past the issue of Black women having white lovers.

In the group, we thought that we would invite Audre when she came to Brandeis, which we did. And it fell apart. Audre wrote this poem, "Women in Trains," afterward for Angela and Jinny. It's in her collection. It's called that because she came from New York on a train.

But I remember, for a long time, I made the decision that no matter what, I would teach Audre. And so she has had a very profound influence on me. I remember going to the Cambridge women's bookstore and seeing all the queer books – they weren't called "queer" then. Those books were at the back. And I remember walking to the back of the bookstore and seeing *Zami: A New Spelling of My Name*. Of course, at the time when I grew up in Trinidad, that word was pejorative, and there she is claiming it. Claiming it's a new spelling of her name. *This is who I am. This is how I want to be known.* To think, then, of honoring her before she took her transit, for me, was one of the most important things I've done in my life. To think of bringing the constituencies together as she had imagined or those that imagined themselves through her. Bringing those communities together was one of the singular most important things I've done politically.

She's right here, you know. I have an altar right here. She and Toni, and a few others are right here. She's never far.

That's the thing about Women's Studies: it needs to think about itself as a political project. It's a political project.

Beverly talked about being in that audience and what that moment was. Those are things that you weave your life around. Those kinds of moments, you weave your life around them.

BGS: The first close Black queer friend I had was Ruby Sales, who happened to have been teaching for a year at Spelman in the History department. This was before the Women's Resource and Research Center was founded. She and I became friends. She was friends with Audre. She invited Audre to Spelman and Audre was treated very badly. I think that Audre was the first out, queer person who had ever spoken at Spelman College. And there was even a Black woman who was a Political Science professor who called me into her office to chastise me for being associated with Audre's visit to campus. I was just stunned.

When Johnnetta Cole came in 1987, she mentioned that Audre had talked to her about her experience at Spelman. And Johnnetta said, "I'm going to get Audre to come to campus." It was because of her friendship with Johnnetta that she came back.

And I will never forget this. We were in the President's House and a student came out as lesbian in front of us. She started crying and Audre pulled her over and hugged her. I'd never seen something like that. I knew that night that the Women's Center would have to be the place on campus where lesbian students would not just be tolerated, but have a space they could call home. Even though, at that point, we didn't have any queer folks in the Women's Center. I would say the mission of the Women's Center was very much shaped by Audre. We were going to be feminist, but it had to also be LGBTQ-friendly. But not just LGBTQ-friendly, it had to put LGBTQ at the center, particularly at a southern Black Christian HBCU [Historically Black College or University], which was quite comfortable with itself. The Women's Center wouldn't be what it is if Audre hadn't passed through there, and Johnnetta. I was committed to making sure that no student would have to cry in isolation because she was at a place where she was treated badly.

MJA: That's profound. That's the piece, right? That's the thinking. You do the politics, and you utilize the insights and the knowledge and experience of those who, at any given moment, could be the most marginalized.

BGS: Yes. Yes.

MJA: That becomes the Center.

BGS: I see you, Briona, as a daughter of the work that Jacqui and Audre and I did and are doing. You are the next generation.

BSJ: I certainly place myself in that lineage. Even when you, Jacqui, were saying that assessing who might be the most marginalized and then building your politics from the ground up – that is an ethics of Black Feminism, but also, I think, an imperative that Audre taught me. I'm living within the continuum that you all created. That relation and continuum was the basis of why I created my anthology, *Mouths of Rain*. Thinking about the anthologies that I read that were not only central to my intellectual and political life, but to my living. And so, I am honored to be your daughter and to continue doing the work.

Contributor Biographies

M. Jacqui Alexander is Professor Emeritus in the Women and Gender Studies Department of the University of Toronto. Previously, Alexander taught at Lang College and was the Wangari Maathai Chair of the Department of Women's and Gender Studies at Connecticut College in New London, Connecticut. While there, she turned what had been an interdisciplinary certificate program into an official major and minor. She also organized a series of conferences featuring multiracial feminist scholars, including Dionne Brand, Chrystos, Angela Y. Davis, Cherrí Moraga, Adrienne Rich, Sonia Sanchez, and Mitsuye Yamada. In 2007, through a grant from the Social Sciences and Humanities Council of Canada, Alexander spent time at Spelman College, where she offered courses that explored the effects of globalization and displacement on the spiritual communities of Aboriginal, African, and African-descendant women, and the spiritual technologies they used to heal themselves and their communities. In 2013, through collaboration between the Community Arts Practice Certificate Program and Faculty of Environmental Studies at York University, in conjunction with Women and Gender Studies at the University of Toronto, Alexander delivered a lecture to kick off a series of events dedicated to the legacies of Audre Lorde. Alexander co-edited *Feminist Genealogies, Colonial Legacies, Democratic Futures* with Chandra Talpade Mohanty and *Sing, Whisper, Shout, Pray! Feminist Visions for a Just World* with Lisa Albrecht, Sharon Day, and Mab Segrest. She is also author of the highly influential *Pedagogies of Crossing: Meditations on Feminism, Sexual Politics, Memory and the Sacred* and of numerous papers, such as "Not Just (Any) Body Can Be a Citizen: The Politics of Law Sexuality and Postcoloniality in Trinidad and Tobago and the Bahamas." Alexander is also the creator and director of the Tobago Centre for the Study and Practice of Indigenous Spirituality.

Jane Anna Gordon is Professor of Political Science at University of Connecticut, Storrs, with affiliations in American Studies, El Instituto, Philosophy, and Women's, Gender, and Sexuality Studies. She is author of *Statelessness and Contemporary Enslavement* (Routledge, 2020), *Creolizing Political Theory* (Fordham University Press, 2014), and *Why They Couldn't Wait* (RoutledgeFalmer, 2001), co-author of *Of Divine Warning* (Routledge, 2009), and co-editor of *Creolizing Rosa Luxemburg* (Rowman & Littlefield, 2021), *The Politics of Richard Wright* (University Press of Kentucky, 2019), *Journeys in Caribbean Thought* (Rowman and Littlefield International, 2016), *Creolizing Rousseau* (Rowman and Littlefield International, 2015), *A Companion to African-American Studies* (Blackwell, 2006), and *Not Only the Master's Tools* (Routledge, 2006). President of the Caribbean Philosophical Association (CPA) from 2014-2017, Gordon continues to direct the CPA Summer School and to co-edit the organization's two book series, *Creolizing the Canon* and *Global Critical Caribbean Studies*. With Lewis Gordon, she is Executive Editor of the new, open access journal *Philosophy and Global Affairs*.

Sula Gordon is a multimedia artist who works as an Admissions Counselor at Parsons School of Design, The New School. Her most recent artist residency was at Carrizozo AIR, in Carrizozo, New Mexico. Through Gordon's paints, prints, and whatever else she can get her hands on, she creates the world she sees and the world she wants to see. Focusing on healing, she refutes the fetishization of Black pain, fighting back against the idea that blackness is only pain. Her work is a love letter to herself, her family, and her community, telling them that their beauty is valuable and seen. More work by Gordon can be found at sulagordon.com.

Beverly Guy-Sheftall, current president of the National Women's Studies Association, is founding director of the Women's Research and Resource Center (created 1981) and Anna Julia Cooper Professor of Women's Studies at Spelman College. Guy-Sheftall has published a number of texts within African American and Women's Studies, including the first anthology on Black women's literature, *Sturdy Black Bridges: Visions of Black Women in Literature* (Doubleday, 1979), which she co-edited with Roseann P. Bell and Bettye Parker Smith; her dissertation, *Daughters of Sorrow: Attitudes Toward Black Women, 1880-1920* (Carlson, 1991); *Words of Fire: An Anthology of African American Feminist Thought* (New Press, 1995); and an anthology she co-edited with Rudolph P. Byrd entitled *Traps: African American Men on Gender and Sexuality* (Indiana University Press, 2001). Her most recent publication is a co-authored monograph, with Johnnetta Betsch Cole, *Gender Talk: The Struggle for Equality in African American Communities,* which was published by Random House in 2003. Upcoming publications include an Oxford University Press anthology of Audre Lorde's writings edited with Rudolph P. Byrd and Johnnetta Betsch Cole. Guy-Sheftall provided leadership for the establishment of the first Women's Studies major at a historically Black college. In her role as Director of Spelman's Women's Center, she has also been involved with the development of student activism around misogynist images of Black women in hip hop and a broad range of social justice issues, including reproductive rights and violence against women. Beyond the academy, she has been involved in the National Black Women's Health Project, the National Council for Research on Women, and the National Coalition of 100 Black Women, on whose boards she has served.

Briona Simone Jones is Assistant Professor of English and Women's, Gender, and Sexuality Studies at the University of Connecticut. She is the editor of the multi-award-winning book *Mouths of Rain: An Anthology of Black Lesbian Thought,* the most comprehensive anthology centering Black Lesbian Thought to date. Jones is currently a Scholar-in-Residence at the Schomburg Center for Research in Black Culture working on her second book, *Black Lesbian Aesthetics.*

Audre Lorde (1934-1992) defined herself as "black, lesbian, feminist, socialist, mother, warrior, poet." Born in Harlem to Caribbean parents, she published nine volumes of poetry (including *Coal* and *The Black Unicorn*), five works of prose (including *The Cancer Journals* and *Sister Outsider*), and a biomythography (*Zami: A New Spelling of My Name*). Consistently challenging racism, homophobia, ableism, and failures to attend to questions of class within the U.S. feminist movement, Lorde taught at Tougaloo College, Lehman College, John Jay College of Criminal Justice, Hunter College, and the Free University of Berlin. Lorde was a transnationalist feminist who framed all forms of oppression as linked by the expressed hostility to difference at their core. Insisting that difference was an indispensable resource and asset in the building of new forms of power and community, she was a consistent and generous supporter to younger scholars and writers. With Barbara Smith, she co-founded Kitchen Table: Women of Color Press to provide infrastructure for Black feminist lesbian writers. Lorde had abiding interests in the global nature of anti-black violence and understood that Black feminist organizing and coalition-building were necessary to the conception and pursuit of liberation.

Elva Orozco Mendoza teaches Political Science and Women's, Gender, and Sexuality Studies at UCONN. A 2020 Junior Faculty Fellow at The Institute for Citizens & Scholars, her work has been published in *Theory and Event, New Political Science, The Journal of Latin American Perspectives*, and *Philosophy and Global Affairs*. Orozco Mendoza is currently completing a book manuscript where she theorizes the concept of the maternal contract.

Sherry Zane is Interim Director of Women's, Gender, and Sexuality Studies at UCONN, which has quadrupled the size of its faculty under her leadership. In 2018 she published "'I did it for the Uplift of Humanity and the Navy': Same-Sex Acts and the Origins of the National Security State, 1919-1921" (*New England Quarterly*) and is currently co-authoring (with Elva Orozco Mendoza and Bhakti Shringarpure) a grant-funded book titled *Insurgent Murals*, on feminist insurgent murals in Argentina, Northern Ireland, and Sudan. She is the recipient of numerous grants and awards, including the Affirming Multivocal Humanities, Mellon Grant; Zoe Blevins Excellence in Allyship Award, Native American Cultural Programs, 2023; CLAS Summer Research Grant, 2022; Department of the Year Award, UConn Rainbow Center, 2022; UConn Leadership Fellows Award, 2021-2022; American Studies Faculty Fellowship, 2021; 2020 Outstanding Teaching and Classroom Inclusion Award, UConn Rainbow Center; and the Franklin and Eleanor Roosevelt Institute Fellowship for Research, 2000.

Also from Daraja Press

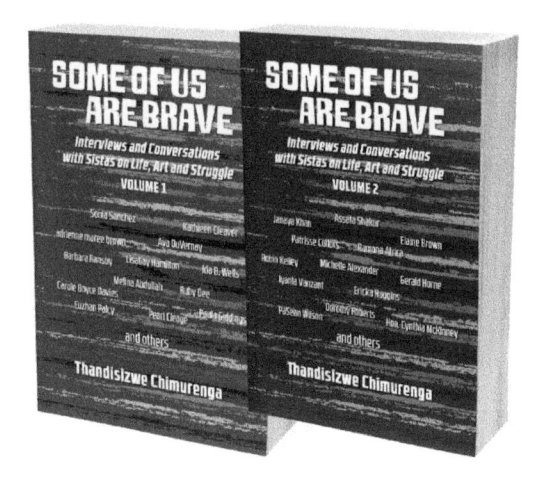

Some Of Us Are Brave, Vols. 1 and 2
Thandisizwe Chimurenga

A society born of white supremacy and patriarchy must, by definition, ignore the voices of Black women. We know that unfortunately, such an attitude will also naturally seep into every stratum of that society

Part of the contribution to correct that was the centering and airing of Black women's voices through Some of Us Are Brave: A Black Women's Radio Program that aired on Pacifica's Los Angeles radio station (KPFK) from 2003 until 2011.

The program covered a myriad of issues by amplifying the voices of a broad cross-section of Black women. Some of those voices have been preserved here in this volume. In addition to capturing various moments in time with a variety of women, this is also a means of taking the intellectual production of and about Black women out of the hands of institutions that are both fundamentally anti-Black and anti-woman.

Volume 1 contains interviews under the headings The Shoulders on Which We Stand and Black Lives Have Always Mattered.

Volume 2 covers Black Women's Health, Bruthas on Sistas, and Sistas in Struggle.

Vol. 1: ISBN-13: 978-1-990263-11-8 • 258 pages • $23
Vol. 2: ISBN-13: 978-1-990263-83-5• 208 pages • $23

Order from **darajapress.com** or **zandgraphics.com**
Prices in U.S. dollars

Daraja Press

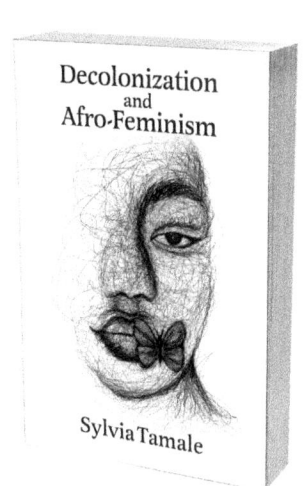

Decolonization and Afro-Feminism
Sylvia Tamale
Winner of the 2022 FTGS Book Prize

In *Decolonization and Afro-Feminism*, Sylvia Tamale provides a powerful guide towards the elimination of two interconnected challenges in contemporary Africa by situating her text as "part of the narrative that does not simply commit to the struggle for decolonization, but also recognizes the dynamics of gender within the struggle for new ways of being".

ISBN-13: 978-1-988832-49-4 • 278 pages • $30

Black Anarchism and the Black Radical Tradition: Moving Beyond Racial Capitalism
Atticus Bagby-Williams & Nsambu Za Suekama

This book shows how hierarchical principles within the Black Panther Party and Black Liberation Army helped generate the emergence of Black anarchism, and breaks new ground in demonstrating that Black anarchism has emerged not only from the European/North American anarchist traditions but rather from roots in Pan-Africanism. The book also highlights concrete, contemporary implications for revolutionary strategy.

ISBN-13: 978-1-990263-32-3 • 62 pages • $18

Insurgent Feminisms: Writing War
Bhakti Shringarpure, Veruska Cantelli

Insurgent Feminisms: Writing War brings together ten years of writing published by *Warscapes* magazine. These perspectives on war come out of regions and positions that defy stereotypical war reportage or the expected war story that come out of regions and positions that defy stereotypical war reportage. *Insurgent Feminisms* comprises reportage, fiction, memoir, poetry and conversations from over sixty writers.

ISBN-13: 978-1-990263-94-1 • 542 pages • $35